At Least Some PR (HOA Edition)

At Least Some PR Because...

Big corporations have whole teams of people handling PR and communication, figuring out something to say when something must be said. When things go wrong.

Homeowner associations, on the other hand, usually can't spend homeowners' money on PR and communication. "PR firms charge anywhere from $5,000 to $10,000/month...paying for PR is absolutely crazy," says Neil St. Clair in a March 2015 *Forbes* article.

Because of cost and other factors, PR is a nonstarter for HOAs. So what happens when there's trouble? When angry homeowners are peppering the board or property manager with difficult questions about thorny issues, or even worse, when HOAs for some reason make headline news?

Well, here's *At Least Some PR*.

In these pages there are examples of hypothetical questions and answers about hypothetical HOA issues. We talk about a cornerstone of PR strategy, anticipating potential issues and problems. There are observations about PR planning, written and verbal communication, neighbor relations, privacy issues and more.

This is PR and communication briefly. It's easy, quick reading because HOA board and committee members have a life. Who wants to plow through volumes of information when you're volunteering time for your HOA?

Table of Contents

(Chapter 1)   Why PR? Because Stuff Happens

Situations and circumstances can change in a heartbeat.

Everything's going great one minute. Then something that seemed just fine, for some bizarre, unexpected reason, suddenly is not okay.

Like, for example, when a major East Coast women's college was suddenly accused of "fat-shaming.".

The college had to apologize for a student health initiative. According to *CBS This Morning*, the college sent "e-mails to students identified as overweight. The messages that invited them to join a program to shed pounds were sent with the intention of raising awareness about health risks associated with being overweight, but the idea backfired and the liberal arts college is now being accused of 'fat-shaming.'"

And remember when suddenly out of nowhere, deflated footballs overshadowed the 2014 Super Bowl?

Even casual, off-the-cuff remarks can go viral. Politicians, business executives, actors, athletes and others say something off the cuff that comes back to haunt them. And some unfortunate something said or done by someone affiliated with a homeowner association -- someone on the board or a committee -- causes confusion, misunderstanding and angst.

And with lots of people -- board members, committee volunteers and others -- often speaking on behalf of HOAs, communication can be discordant, confusing and misunderstood. Someone's on one page while someone else is on an entirely different page.

(Chapter 2)   PR Boiled Down

Trying to anticipate potential issues is what PR is all about. What if this or that happens?

PR professionals often start conversations with the word -- **_SUPPOSE_**.

That's PR, it's a lot of hypothetical thinking.

This hypothetical thinking, this mental exercise, serves an important purpose. As they anticipate issues, PR people formulate an initial response to anticipated questions.

This is a starting point, an immediate, often very general, response to questions about almost anything that might occur. So if questions are raised about this, that or whatever, there's something on paper or in the computer...and available on the shelf if some initial response is necessary.

PR communication -- or messaging, as PR people like to say -- can help clarify situations and, equally important, buy some time. A general response can do that...it can buy a little time when there's a need to step back, to take a breath, to further evaluate whatever's going on. It's a process for anticipating and initially managing issues.

(Chapter 3)   Thorny HOA Issues

So let's look at potential HOA issues and hypothetical questions and answers for addressing issues. You'll see as you're reading that some of the answers in the Q&A are so general -- so broad-brush -- they can sometimes be recycled. An answer for one particular question about one particular issue may also serve as a response for other questions about other issues.

And as you're reading *At Least Some PR*, keep this...this...this...and this in mind:

- That one size does not fit all community associations. HOAs have their unique characteristics, unique governing documents, rules, regulations, procedures and circumstances.

- That HOAs may need a qualified, professional property manager's counsel or legal counsel from a qualified attorney for guidance in addressing -- and responding to -- various issues. And that circumstances may necessitate that a property manager or attorney act as the spokesperson for an HOA..

- Also keep in mind that PR is not an exact science. PR professionals attempt to anticipate issues and develop communication for addressing issues, but outcomes may vary.

(Chapter 4)   Let's Suppose...Some Q&A

Suppose homeowners install over-the-top decor on and all around their home, to celebrate holidays, for example. They put up thousands of bright lights and decorations. The display is so bright and dazzling that it just might be visible to astronauts in orbit circling the Earth.

Thousands of onlookers stopping by at night block sidewalks and neighbors' driveways and cause traffic snarls and other problems. Candy wrappers, soda cans and other debris litter the neighborhood.

Distressed neighbors contact the property manager. A really fed up homeowner alerts local TV stations and newspapers about all the commotion.

Neighbors and reporters ask these questions:

(Q)   What's the HOA's policy? What are you planning to do about this?

Here's a hypothetical, very general answer:

(A)   We hope to be able to address this situation through discussions involving the homeowner, the homeowners association and concerned neighbors.

(Q)   Do you have policies that would apply?

(A)   Resolving this through discussions between the homeowner, concerned neighbors and the association is the goal and preferred outcome. Without going into details, if it becomes necessary, there are policies for addressing matters of this nature.

Keep This in Mind -- If pressed to provide details about "policies for addressing matters of this nature," the response might be: This is all I have to say at this time.

Complex, Emotional Issues

Now suppose there's a big brouhaha because a fictional board president opens this fictional HOA's meetings with a prayer?

Some homeowners voice concerns:

(Q) I don't practice religion. Why should I be subjected to prayers when I attend an HOA meeting?

(A) Thank you for bringing this to our attention. We will look into this matter.

Keep This in Mind -- A very general response like this may be all that can be said, especially in response to inquiries about a complex, emotional issue. Professional PR people would want to be sure there is follow-up addressing a sensitive issue like this, that somehow the issue can be resolved. And with issues of this nature, counsel provided by a qualified, professional property manager or HOA attorney may be necessary.

Showing the Flag(s)

Many large, national flags are being displayed at a homeowner's property. Since this may be in violation of the HOA's governing documents and neighbors are complaining about the flags, the homeowner is asked to remove them.

Citing patriotism, the homeowner complains to the association's property manager and the board and takes this issue to the news media. Resulting in this question from a TV news reporter:

(Q)   Why would you force someone to remove patriotic flags?

(A)   We're aware of concerns about the flags, primarily involving the number of flags displayed and the size of flags. We will discuss this with the homeowner and neighbors expressing concerns, with the goal of achieving a resolution of this situation.

<u>Keep This in Mind</u> -- A very general comment like this may buy some time for thorough evaluation of a complex issue like this. Sometimes there's little to be gained from engaging in a lengthy discussion or debate. But again, this reminder that issues and circumstances vary...they can be fluid. And of course, if there are potential legal issues, legal counsel by a qualified attorney may be necessary.

What a Dues-zy!!

When a homeowners association increases homeowners' monthly assessments (or dues), angry homeowners complain.

(Q)   Aren't we paying enough? How can you justify raising our dues?

(A)   With the cost of ongoing and long-term maintenance and upgrades of our HOA in mind, it's necessary to increase monthly assessments at this time. Ensuring sufficient funding for our HOA community is important and necessary, not just for today, but for the years ahead, as well.

While at times it becomes necessary to increase the monthly assessment to further build funding, we also evaluate options for reducing the assessment in accordance with changing operational and funding needs.

Keep This in Mind -- Before using a statement like this, it's important to know that HOA leaders are indeed committed to adjusting assessments up or down in accordance with funding needs. A response must reflect reality.

And This Dues-zy!

Now suppose word is going around that a homeowner is extremely delinquent paying monthly association dues. Homeowners complain...Hey! Everyone else pays dues on time.

(Q)   How can you allow this to happen?

(A)   Out of respect for the privacy of everyone residing in our Association -- for all homeowners -- we're not able to comment on inquiries of this nature.

<u>Keep This in Mind</u> -- Before using even a 'No comment' statement like this, for sensitive matters involving privacy issues, you may need counsel provided by a qualified, professional property manager or HOA attorney.

Get Outta My Face!

Now suppose several board members get into a shoving match during a heated debate. Or board members and homeowners engage in shoving or other such behavior. Bystanders attending the meeting are appalled.

(Q)   What's going on? How can this behavior be condoned?

(A)   Every effort is made to amicably resolve disagreements that may occur during meetings.

<u>Keep This in Mind</u> -- A general response like this may calm heated emotions. But, again, this reminder: That professional PR people would want to be sure there really is a commitment to amicably resolve disagreements before communicating a response like this.

Favoritism?

An angry homeowner alleges that the board is showing favoritism toward certain homeowners, leading to this hypothetical question:

(Q)   Shouldn't everyone -- all homeowners -- be treated fairly and equally?

(A)   Thank you for your inquiry. Addressing matters in an objective manner is the board's goal.

<u>Keep This in Mind</u> -- Again, before using a statement like this, be sure that HOA leadership is committed to objectivity and fairness in addressing homeowners' needs. The neat thing about PR is that, along with shaping communication about issues, PR can sometimes generate positive thinking and positive practices.

Oh Come On! Of Course I Can!

A homeowner lodges a complaint regarding an architectural change request that has been declined by the association's architectural committee.

(Q)   Why can't I add a room to my home since the addition I have in mind will not be visible to my neighbors?

(A)   The information about our homeowner association provided to homeowners (the governing documents) includes details about architectural modifications. The association is not able to approve proposed modifications that are not in compliance with architectural requirements. There may be other authorized options that you may want to consider.

Keep This in Mind -- Since governing documents vary among community associations, you would need to be sure that a general response like this reflects the architectural policies detailed in your HOA's governing documents.

We Demand to Know!

There's gossip that a homeowner is suing the association for a considerable amount of money. Several owners who are concerned about the potential cost demand that the property manager or board disclose information about the rumored lawsuit.

Keep This in Mind -- Legal counsel may be absolutely necessary for determining if there can be any response to inquiries regarding potential, pending or existing legal matters. In business, often a 'no comment' or 'I'm sorry, I'm not able to provide information.' is the only comment that can be made about legal issues.

Why Should I?

A homeowner who frequently hosts gatherings in a common area of the HOA refuses to clean up litter left by guests, arguing that homeowner dues should pay for common area maintenance. The homeowner complains to the board.

(Q)   I'm already paying a lot each month. Why should I have to clean the common area?

(A)   While monthly homeowner dues (or assessments) fund a range of HOA maintenance needs, they do not cover costs associated with the removal of litter resulting from social gatherings. We're grateful to everyone for their efforts to pick up their litter after using the HOA's recreational facilities and common areas.

Can't I, Just a Little Longer?

Several residents are questioning the HOA's guest parking policy, wondering why residents can only keep their cars in guest parking spaces for specified hours or a specified number of days before they have to move their vehicles.

(Q)   Why can't homeowners keep their vehicles in the extra parking spaces in our HOA?

(A)   Guest parking is needed for people visiting HOA residents and for contractors and others doing work at residents' homes and providing maintenance services for the association. As an accommodation, residents can park in guest spaces for the designated time.

Is the Smoking Lamp Lit?

(Q) **What is the association's policy on smoking and second-hand smoke issues?**

(A) Such issues, if they occur, would be addressed on a case-by-case basis.

<u>Keep This in Mind</u> -- This is a very general comment regarding a potentially complex issue. Also, various associations may have smoking policies established in governing documents or there may be local or state laws on smoking. You may need counsel provided by a qualified, professional property manager or HOA attorney.

Way Too Harsh?

A homeowner who is months behind paying HOA dues is denied access to HOA recreational facilities. The angry homeowner asks:

(Q) **Why is this penalty so excessive and unfair? Why would any homeowner be treated in such a shabby manner?**

(A) Thank you for bringing your concerns to our attention. The regular assessments paid by homeowners are extremely important. They provide the funding needed for ongoing and long-term operations and maintenance of the HOA. Because this funding is so important, it's our goal to monitor and address matters involving regular assessments.

<u>Keep This in Mind</u> -- This hypothetical response includes observations about funding for ongoing and long-term HOA needs that may not be top of mind for homeowners.

Eye in the Sky

A neighbor is flying drones with cameras onboard, often in close proximity to homes throughout this fictional HOA neighborhood. Concerned residents lodge complaints with the property manager...We're concerned about our privacy and the danger caused by drones zooming through our neighborhood.

(Q) What are you going to do about this?

(A) It's important, initially, to discuss this with the individual who is operating the drones, to communicate the concerns that are being expressed. With anything new and novel, this initial step is important, along with addressing situations of this nature on a case-by-case basis.

<u>Keep This in Mind</u> -- General comments like this can buy time for a thorough evaluation of a complex issue. Also, HOA governing documents and local, state or federal laws may apply. Counsel provided by a qualified attorney may be necessary.

Charge it!

An HOA property manager is getting inquiries about electric vehicle charging stations.

(Q) Is the HOA planning to install charging stations? If not, why not?

(A) With anything new and novel -- rapidly-evolving technology, for example -- it's important and necessary to thoroughly evaluate options.

<u>Keep This in Mind</u> -- Various laws or regulations at municipal and state levels may apply to vehicle charging stations.

How About Red? Or Green? Or Blue, Maybe?

Several homeowners complain to the property manager about painting maintenance for HOA homes (this fictional association is responsible for -- and funds -- exterior painting maintenance). The concerned homeowners want entirely different paint colors for homes. But in this example, with cost factors in mind, there's a preference to stick with the existing color scheme.

(Q) We've had the same color scheme on our homes for a long time, isn't it time for a change?

(A) Your views regarding painting maintenance are much appreciated.

With the funding currently allocated for this project in mind, painting homes in the existing colors is a cost-effective option for homeowners. Cost is a key consideration for projects, since costs associated with HOA maintenance, upgrades and operational needs are funded by homeowners through their ongoing, regular assessments.

(Q) Does this mean we'll never be able to change the color scheme for our homes?

(A) The color scheme can be changed. But this would likely necessitate building additional funding to cover costs associated with a color scheme change.

Harassment Allegations

A homeowner alleges harassment by several directors on the board who allegedly make demeaning remarks about the homeowner. The owner asks the HOA's property manager:

(Q) What is the association going to do about this?

(A) Thank you for bringing this to our attention. We will discuss this with the board.

<u>Keep This in Mind</u> -- When you say you're going to discuss a matter like this with the board, it's important to keep the commitment.

Street Maintenance Angst

Work on streets maintained by this fictional HOA is being scheduled and homeowners along the streets aren't thrilled.

(Q)   You're going to be repairing our street...what an inconvenience that we won't be able to access our driveways. Couldn't this have been better planned?

(The response, below, is based on the HOA or the street repair contractor providing residents with helpful information about the planned maintenance.)

(A)   While necessary street maintenance is underway, our neighbors in the area where work is being done will not be able to access their driveways. In the notification regarding this work, information about temporary, alternative parking was provided. Every attempt is being made to minimize inconvenience during the course of this maintenance work.

Congregating Congregation

What started out as a small group of people getting together for a prayer service at the home of a fictional resident of a fictional HOA has grown to a substantial number of people attending regularly-scheduled services.

With such a large number of people gathering each week at the home, neighbors are complaining about noise and traffic problems. They feel that a residential neighborhood is not the place to conduct regularly-scheduled services. The HOA doesn't allow homeowners to run a commercial business out of their home, why should these large public meetings be condoned?

But the fictional homeowner hosting the prayer services sees things differently. Citing religious freedom, the homeowner vows to continue holding the weekly meetings.

A local TV station contacts the property manager seeking

comment about this dispute between neighbors. Here's the reporter's questions:

(Q)   With religious freedom in mind, how will your HOA address this dispute?

(A)   The objective is to achieve an amicable resolution of this situation. What that will be remains to be determined.

(Q)   But doesn't religious freedom make this more complicated and more difficult to resolve?

(A)   As mentioned, the objective is an amicable resolution. What that will be remains to be determined.

<u>Keep This in Mind</u> -- Because of the complexity of this hypothetical situation, the initial response is very general. Counsel provided by a qualified property manager and/or HOA attorney may be necessary. Also...there have been some court decisions in matters of this nature.

(Chapter 5)   Interesting, isn't it?

Interesting, isn't it? Anticipating issues. Sometimes this mental exercise can be as easy as compiling two lists, with potential HOA issues, concerns and problems detailed in one of the lists. And the values received by everyone residing in the HOA -- all the good things -- noted in the second list.

Brutal honesty is the best policy. The values should be tangible and not just PR fluff. The issues, concerns, etc. should be the real thing too, even if you have to grit your teeth as you're writing them down.

When you anticipate thoroughly and honestly, you can be better prepared to deal with potential problems. Or even better, you can sometimes avoid problems all together.

(Chapter 6)   Speaking of Avoiding Problems...

It's jokingly called foot-in-mouth disease, but it's no joke when words race ahead of thoughts. Just ask people forced to mea culpa their way out of trouble caused by unfortunate verbal communication, or these days, unfortunate email or text messages. Such communication isn't necessarily private.

Must every utterance be planned, orchestrated, rehearsed? Or would it be easier to simply press a 'pause' button in your mind?

Even PR professionals in pressure cooker moments of TV, radio and print media interviews are okay with an occasional pause -- a little dead air time -- to be sure they aren't releasing words ahead of thoughts.

Even when there's a barrage of homeowners' questions and commentary during a board meeting, consider pressing your mental 'pause' button.

A little silence, a little dead air time, is often preferable to an ill-conceived response. Or when issues are so complex that an immediate response just isn't possible, the board or property manager can explain the need to give thought to issues or concerns raised by homeowners. As long as there's follow-through, it can be okay to get back to homeowners, when necessary.

(Chapter 7)   Oh Sh---t!!
You Answer Your Phone and It's a Newspaper or TV Reporter...

This may seem easier said than done, but staying reasonably calm is what PR professionals would try to do. They would listen closely to what the reporter is saying and asking. Listening is important.

They might try to buy some time if there's a need to consider what to do. By perhaps telling a reporter...*I'll need to get back to you.* Since reporters are generally on a deadline for filing stories, it's seldom possible to buy a lot of time. But even a little time is better than nothing.

Buying time can provide an opportunity to touch base with others who may be able to help determine a prudent course of action.

When a reporter contacts the president of an HOA board, for example, the board president may want to reach out to the HOA's property manager or attorney...or a PR professional if the association or its property management company uses PR and communication services.

And then, if everything quickly falls in place, a strategy for dealing with the reporter's inquiry can be worked out.

(Chapter 8)　Now, Here's More in Excerpts From Our Other booklet, *HOA Over Easy*

Proactive Communication...Good Neighbor Relations

Much can be said about getting out in front of issues. For example, proactively explaining a decision to remove trees in a common area because the trees are diseased can address residents' questions and concerns.

Everyone Plays a Role in PR

Everyone participating in HOA management -- HOA volunteers and property managers, for example -- is, in a sense, the face of the association.

A number of factors can influence opinion of community associations...for example:

- The perception of value received when residing in a community association

- The manner in which inquiries, issues and concerns are addressed

- Perception of HOA governance and leadership

- Perception of community association communication

Through clear, informative communication, HOA leaders can discuss the association's role, its goals and initiatives.

 Communication helps generate understanding and buy-in. It helps avoid misunderstanding.

Avoiding misunderstandings and problems is far preferable to unwinding them. Spending time, energy and resources fixing things is wasteful, counterproductive and costly.

Ensuring a timely response to homeowner inquiries is also important. And when, for whatever reason, it isn't possible to provide an immediate response, letting homeowners know their inquiries will be addressed within a reasonable time is important.

Word choice in verbal and written communication can either calm things down or stir things up.

Sensitive Stuff and Privacy

As an elected representative on the HOA board or as a volunteer serving on a committee, you may be privy to sensitive matters between neighbors and the association. For example as an architectural committee member, you may have information about a homeowner's architectural change request.

You may be aware of legal matters and legal communication involving homeowners. Such information is in the private domain. Virtually everything involving homeowners and the association should be considered private.

Even concerns or complaints raised during the course of informal conversations between board members, committee volunteers and homeowners should be considered private.

In conversations and all communication -- letters, emails, etc. -- privacy should be seen as a top priority.

(Chapter 9)   Last but not Least, Sample Articles for HOA Media.

A Worthy Goal...Living in Harmony

While bickering on reality shows and among politicians may be the norm these days, our HOA community can be a bickering-free zone. It just takes a little LU...a little listening and understanding.

Listening to neighbors' concerns, issues or misunderstandings. Spending a little time assessing situations, rather than making snap judgments.

Living in harmony involves respect for neighbors and the HOA neighborhood. By putting everything back in order after spending time in a recreational facility, for example...straightening furniture you've used and using refuse containers.

And being sure that people visiting your home know where to park their cars, so they aren't blocking access to a neighbor's home. And when entertaining guests, keeping sound at a reasonable level.

It's these little things that can make a big difference, so that everyone can fully enjoy their community association.

Who Me? Why Would I Want to be on the Board?

Why serve? To share your expertise while gaining new insights and knowledge.

There's more to HOAs than meets the eye.

There's infrastructure...the common areas and recreational facilities and everything needed to maintain infrastructure. There's irrigation and lighting systems, common area sidewalks and streets, and more.

Participating in the management of HOA infrastructure is challenging in a positive way. Along with participating in HOA financial management.

Working to ensure sufficient funding for ongoing operational needs, as well as long-term maintenance and upgrades is interesting and challenging.

HOAs are multi-faceted, multi-million-dollar communities. Participating in financial management can be comparable to earning a mini-MBA degree.

Conclusion

At Least Some PR, as the title suggests, is a little something about PR. But sometimes, more than a little something may be needed for sorting out particularly complex, thorny situations. Just as, under certain circumstances, counsel provided by a qualified, professional property manager or qualified HOA attorney may be necessary, PR counsel may be necessary in particularly challenging circumstances.

For more information about *At Least Some PR*, contact: hoastrategic@gmail.com

About the Author

Harvey Radin admits to being a PR wonk.

After he retired as a corporate communications executive for Bank of America in Los Angeles, London, New York and San Francisco, he was a PR, media relations and crisis communications consultant for other large and mid-tier financial firms and consumer product companies.

His articles about communication, public opinion and PR have been published in American Banker, Business Insider, PR media and regional newspapers

www.ingramcontent.com/pod-product-compliance
Lightning Source LLC
Chambersburg PA
CBHW070849180526
45168CB00009B/1659